When I Got Drunk with My Mother

Also by Shelley Townsend-Hudson

When I Got Drunk with My Mother
Into
From the Window
This Southern Thing about Shoes
Paths before We Knew Them
Hibriten
Companions for the Soul (with Robert Hudson)

When I Got Drunk with My Mother

Poems about Growing Up Southern

Shelley Townsend-Hudson

PERKIPERY PRESS / CHAPBOOK PRESS
2020

Chapbook Press

Schuler Books
2660 28th Street SE
Grand Rapids, MI 49512
(616) 942-7330
www.schulerbooks.com

When I Got Drunk with My Mother

Copyright © 2020 by Shelley Townsend-Hudson

Published in association with the Perkipery Press.

ISBN 13: 9781948237680

Library of Congress Control Number: 2020924384

For inquiries, contact the author at:
    Perkipery Press
    8405 Baileau Oaks Dr. NE
    Ada, MI   49301
    hudsbob@comcast.net

The following poems were first published in *Voices*, a publication of the Dyer-Ives Foundation containing the winners of their annual poetry contest: "Janie" (2005), "My Father's Fancy" (2008), "Down the Road" (2011), and "When I Got Drunk with My Mother" (2016).

Other poems appeared in these chapbooks: *Hibriten* (2004), *Paths before We Knew Them* (2005), *This Southern Thing about Shoes* (2006), *From the Window* (2007), *Into* (2008), and *When I Got Drunk with My Mother* (2010), all available from the Perkipery Press.

Thank you to Tammy Johnson for her gorgeous cover design.

First printing. All rights reserved.

Printed in the United States of America.

In
memory of
Mama
and
Daddy

Introduction

My four sisters and I grew up at the foot of a mountain in North Carolina. Year after year our family saw Hibriten change with the seasons, and morning after morning we watched the sun rise behind it – all from our breakfast table.

At Christmas a huge star still shines at night from its summit. And at Easter, a cross. Several hundred lightbulbs keep these symbols blazing at 2,200 feet above the small furniture-factory town of Lenoir.

In the summertime, so thick was the foliage in our backyard, you wouldn't have known a mountain was there, though my father cleared trails for hiking and horseback riding. But in the fall, this majestic mountain rose above our red barn, above the acres of woodland we called The Far Hill, and it was "as pretty a mountain as any that adorns the earth," as Henry E. Colton describes Hibriten in his 1856 book, *Mountain Scenery*.

We never thought it special or unusual to have a mountain in our backyard. We'd climb it at least once a year, even ride horses to the top. Clambering up the fire tower added an extra measure of thrill to our mountaineering.

Hibriten was constant and ever-present. We lived in its shadow and its shelter, and the poems in this collection sprang from its soil.

– Shelley Townsend-Hudson, December 2020

When I Got Drunk with My Mother

Hibriten

In a flash of lightning, sixty years,
my path narrows with bent dry grass while
the grasshoppers spring ahead of me.

But if I turn I see the mountain near
the place I lived, framed by a window.
And tree frogs still sing in the night.

Baby in a Car, 1956

As the woods swept by, I knocked my chunky
shoes against the dashboard of the Bel Air,
pointed my finger at tall shapes that flickered
by on the sunlit horizon, and twisted my face
up to Mama's, who was looking the other way.

There was no substantial or insubstantial here
on her lap, just quiet movement and light,
giving a fluttering sensation to tall things,
like when I'd let my eyes rove over the slats
of my crib in the dim light of the room.

At first, things existed by imprint, then named
and treasured until everything came together
without the slightest seam. But before then,
trees, when first seen, unlabeled, were strange,
so very, very strange.

New Apples

My daughter asked to see scars
from burns I had received, long ago,
when my nightgown caught fire.

Her younger sister asked, "Did you have
to throw it away?" Funny, how she
comes from the underside of things

like Newton's law: each memory stays at rest
unless compelled by another. It never
occurred to me what my parents

did with a tiny singed gown.
The question took flight, and at its apex
my mother fingers a one-winged

remnant from the back of a drawer
a thousand answers deep, then,
with a sigh, throws it in the bin.

Dog Called Keats

You
 brown
black
white
beagle
flattened out
on a cowskin
rug the color
of liver

my towhead
resting
on your
speckled
belly
rising
falling

Daddy gave
you
to me

I was
three

He said
Shelley
needs a
Keats

And that
is how
I learned
how
to
love

how
to
grieve

how
to curl
myself
into
the
shape of
calm

Maid in the South

Mary Jo
though you had
your own small son
called June Bug
you were still
my second mama.
One Christmas you raved
"What a lot o' presents
for such a little girl"
and that night
when we drove you home
to West End
behind the smokestacks
my cheeks burned
to see June Bug
racing spread-armed
across your gravel
into your arms.

What We Seen

Chaps and vests looped on bedposts
    hula hoops on knobs
we both got jars of lime green light
fireflies on watch tonight

Uncle Frank's come down from Boston
lots of kids came 'round today
he cracked his bullwhip in the summer heat
and we won't get much sleep tonight

We'd headed out to The Red Pig
for the best Bar-B-Q in town
I got dibs on the front seat, Jesus rode on the dash
and our headlights spread out flat

Something glowed like a brushfire ahead
couldn't tell if it was house or woods
my sister and me with necks craned up
were riveted to the burning cross

Chaps and vests looped on bedposts
as we breathed under hot sheets
thinking of the shoutin', the smoke, and the sparks
and just how hushed it got in the car tonight

Landmarks

Our town had two traffic circles,
one on the east side, one in the center.
We'd circle one to get to the Green
Stamp Store and Burger House, the other,

to get to the courthouse, the bank,
or Peterson's Shoes. Men in overalls
slumped on the courthouse stoop.
At Christmas, trees were put up

in the circles. Before entering traffic
you could buy a News Topic, not
much news in the valley, but the sun
spiraled on, day, night, day, night.

Our family had its own landmarks –
Tremont Tree, forked and grinning,
gauging the distance yet to home.
The Crying Tree with a boulder

where we'd sit when sad or angry,
to seek the door in the dark to set
our frightened imaginations free.
As trees and circles greened

year after year we pulled the end
of the golden string to its length
and reeled it back again –
sweet sequence to grant us bearings.

Nostalgia, circa 1959

Minton's had to be the only two-pump station paved in bottle caps, thousands of them, 7up, RC, Tab, Cheerwine, Sun Drop, Pepsi, Brownie, embedded in oil and dirt

The only place in town to buy raw milk Daddy liked it raw. Springing from the car, we felt the caps in the heat, little heartbeats under our feet. It was dark and cool inside

We'd bend in half for a pop from the cooler a Palmer Cox Brownie sign on the wall. We'd pry them open, mash our caps into the mosaic, hoping for a car to roll over them soon

Years later, on a date, my husband and I, hiking, vowed we'd not become attached to things. We buried something on us, a ring, a pen knife. Years later I sent him out to find the ring. So much for resolve

Still, heaven should be paved with bottle caps, leading to loved ones, leaning on a fence. The search for what's true is done, we'll know the place as a long exhalation, where Minton's is forever 'round the corner

Summer in the Fifties

It must've been an odd summer, being quarantined.
My sisters painted their bikes blue with yellow stars,
the City Pool closed, and the Avon, where mice
snagged your popcorn during the show, was off-limits.

A girl got polio anyway. My sisters talked about the iron lung
she lived in – as mysterious to me as the Iron Curtain. Later,
when I saw a book with a man on the cover encased
in an iron lung, my sisters' questions came back:

How did she go to the bathroom? Could she get out? How'd
she eat and sleep? Could she roll over? Itch her nose? Would
she get married? Have children? And what did it sound like
with all that breathing in the house?

Hands

1.

Aunt Lillian had polio but never
got an iron lung. What she did get
was a crumpled hand, a whopsided walk,
and a black Bible heftier than a frying pan.

She'd eye me like she wanted to try my life on
for size, hers being rougher than a cob. Whenever
I squint into the past, I wish I'd talked to her more,
instead of always casting sidelongs at that hand.

2.

Poke, Sloke, Slokum, Inkberry –
whatever you call those wild berries,
you'd be graveyard dead to eat one.
I used to pluck and pulverize them
and stain rocks all day Saturday.

Next morning in our usual pew,
my purple hands sweating in white
gloves, I'd recollect the cool slippery
wet in my palms, trying hard not
to think on long blunt nails.

3.

Early don't last long, my daddy used to say
about how fast we were growing up. Seemed
like only yesterday us kids hunkered on Big
Rock swatting no-see-ums and whining about
the fish not biting. Daddy'd slip, sight unseen,

into the fishing hole, grappling for bream to hook on
our lines. When we'd start hollerin' and reeling in,
he'd glide on the scene, swabbing his hands
on the seat of his pants, praising our catches.

Under the Rug

How did I get so lucky as to witness
a fight between my mother and aunt?
You forget grown-ups can be sisters.

You also forget the devil's in the details,
though I knew my grandmother
factored heavily in them.

At the end my aunt just packed her tiny
suitcase and trudged down the road.
A victim of polio, she had Charlie Chaplin's gait.

Later, when we went looking for her
she loomed up, tilted in the headlights.
But by dang they never did make up.

Why Can't We Be Good

It comes back to me sometimes
that time I was five, coming out
of the bathroom, my sister asking
what took so long. Nonchalantly, I said
I was pulling the legs off a daddy longlegs

Vaguely I remember it was an experiment:
bathroom, my clinic, yellow towel spread,
me, focusing over my specimen.
My sister shamed me. I knew I wasn't
bad just curious and kind of weird

It comes back to me sometimes
mean things I said on the playground
you're a fat pig, you cheat at marbles,
you stole my best ghost marble. You won it
fair and square, I adjusted, we got on

It comes to mind I judge people in their Jesus
T-shirts, pumping gas. I catch myself.
My wise daughter says, it's your second
thought and not your first that's the real you
I guess it comes to this, we're not here long, be good

Burning

I was five when I had scarlet fever
hot as fire in my mama's bed
sheers billowed in the window
in, out, in, out, like breathing,
a floor fan in the corner? Maybe.
Mama and Daddy hovered
their faces looming, they billowed too
big, small, big, small
I remember thinking about a whale
with its one big eye watching me

Next morning, the doctor came
he drew a circle on my tummy
did we play tick-tac-toe?
my tummy was red
his fingernail could draw in white.
He blew up a balloon, rubbed it on my hair
it stuck to the wall above the bed
like magic! Looking back at my parents
caring for me was magic
the love of parents for a child

being very sick and then not sick
well, that was a kind of magic too

Crayola

What's that for? I asked, pointing to a string
with a small loop dangling over a chair.
Daddy looked at me on the floor and explained,
When the nightsitter comes, Namaw has
the girl tie it to her toe. Whenever Namaw
needs the bedpan, she yanks it to wake the sitter.

I studied the crayon apron around my waist,
slots for 48 different colors. I pulled out Prussian
Blue – that's what Namaw said it was called –
and Silver, my favorites and drew the scene.
Toe-yanker, small face, long Gray braid,
bedpan, glowing like the moon, under the bed.

Can we take her on an "amblance" ride again?
The ambulance driver Daddy hired had given us
a color tour. Redbuds, dogwoods, azaleas.
My sister and me in cowboy chaps. Our beagle,
along for the ride, weaving in and out from under
Namaw's shiny bed. Light flickered everywhere, White.

That'd be nice, Daddy replied. I took Keats outside,
he lifted a leg, his nose to the Burnt Sienna ground.
I fished my Indian Red plastic plane from a pocket,

looping the rubber band on a hook, sent it soaring.
Sunlight shimmered through Yellow Green leaves.
How many colors does the light have?

I ran in when the plane took a header on the rooftop.
She died a month later. When we went through her things,
I kept her basket of Scrabble tiles. I was learning my ABCs.
We sold the house. A couple years later we passed by,
and my Indian Red plane was still on her roof.

Eggs

The rooster kept congratulating itself
long after the sun was up.
We made our way to the hen house,
my mother in shirtwaist dress and heels,
and me, at five, with no shirt or shoes.

She reached under to gather eggs,
never mind their protests,
while I dodged droppings.
Why I walked that ground
barefoot, I'll never know.

We'd fill the cartons and deliver them
in town; my job, to jump out,
tote cartons to front stoops and
porches, skipping back with empty ones.
At one house, I'd sometimes find

hard candy in the twelve empty spots.
I never considered how eggs wound
up on tables – scrambled, sunny-side up,
blessed or not. But I can't hear a cock's crow
without remembering shaking empty cartons.

A Bit Ragged and Funny

I'm the leghorn – once a dime-store
Easter chick – who took a chunk out
of your mother's leg. You and your
sister wrestled me into the house for rehab.
Mitch Miller on the Hi-Fi.

On the newel, I surveyed the scene
with red eyes as dull as the music.
Afterwards you drew straws –
who'd clean the droppings? –
before hurling me fan-feathered into the rain.

Primary Class

From First Methodist we walked
with our Christmas baskets to a house
behind the factory, we barely fit
into the living room while the family crowded
on and around the couch, listening
to our carols. An old man with bare feet
in slippers let tears slide down his face. I stood,
in my blue velvet dress, wondering how he got
to be him and me, me. I saw how he could
have been me, how we all might have been another,
and yet breathing the same liver-scented air.

First Grade

Mama took us uptown to Roses,
bought me a plaid satchel –
did I want the red pocket or the black –
you'll need a Blue Horse tablet.

That year Natalie taught me to walk
through the culvert under the road,
we straddled its dark length through
concentric circles, edgy for snakes.

Numbers two and five, I reversed.
They looked the same upside-down.
The E in Esso was a backwards three.
Numbers and letters were odd,

uneven, looping along the edge
of the chalkboard. We followed
with a nervous vigilance as if through
a tunnel; dull Dick and Jane tagging

along with good intentions.
But before ever adhering to outlines,
we knew, first hand, where our best
good treasures lay.

Saturday Pokes

Daddy took us, some Saturdays,
to the courthouse where there
was a whites-only drinking fountain
and a blind man who ran the snack bar
and knew a five-dollar bill by its feel.

At the two-pump station, Daddy let us
fill bags with Pixie sticks, licorice, and
fireballs, but the coveted candy Pall Malls,
we just eyeballed. Daddy himself smoked Kents.

At Seven

I stood in the doorframe, nightgown-clad,
weeping, I was sure I'd die and go to hell while
Mama and Daddy would be in heaven.
What I'd give to see again that slant glance
between them, the nearest to intimacy,
bringing me in.

Attic

Like Jonah's whale, the attic rafters
rose above our summer playhouse
or our stage where disorder
contrasted to expectations downstairs,
where we'd don old clothes to act out
how to live without knowing how.

Like walking sidewalks at night, eyeing families
through windows; we'd try one on,
holding mirrors to the life, while downstairs
Mama scoured and Daddy cleaned
a gun barrel. We opened up our instant lives
and gave full encounters of ourselves.

Blue Budgie

Blue mountain framed by a window
greets me on a sun-filled morning
at the table I scrape Cream of Wheat
till the Currier and Ives scene appears
children swinging on an old farm gate

Our parakeet perches on the faucet
cocking his head this way and that
water rushing beneath his feet
my mama scours the frying pan
and Daddy offers me bacon

Today is Picture Day, I say
and Petey flies a blue-blurred
arc to my shoulder, shuffling
the length of a seam to my neck
and back, I hold my breath

He pecks a brass button on my jumper
then flashes a stink eye, as if to say,
This dent you will see in your third-grade
picture. You'll recall bacon smell,
blue mountain, bird, and bowl,

you'll remember Mama and Daddy
in this recalibrated scene meant
to assure you how exquisitely you were loved
how everything then was what you needed
to make you who you are now

Christmas Star on Hibriten

A great star beamed from the peak
every season. No one to my knowledge
complained about it and only time will tell

Giant Christmas trees stood in traffic circles
at the Crossroads and uptown, not fresh cut,
but boughs that were layered on hoops,

rising higher and higher as you rounded
the circles to school, work, the Five 'n' Dime
or Belks. The traffic circles are gone now

One year my father decided we needed a sprig
of raisins in our stockings, only thing he
got as a boy, that, an orange and some nuts

We'd never seen raisins on the vine, haven't
since, but the message wasn't lost on us
The flimsy cardboard Santa and sleigh display

on the factory rooftop warranted an annual
family drive-by. We sat wide-eyed
in the back, never considering that these

small amazements, like the star – tiara of
an impossibly fat queen – would one day
offer measures of provisional peace

Shooting Down the Mistletoe

Daddy and I took the 12 gauge
and headed to The Far Hill
he carried the gun downward
bits of mica glinted up from the road

An easy quiet between us
we entered woods and found
an oak full of mistletoe
circled it then climbed a rock

He showed me how to aim,
through crosshairs and up through
branches, how to release
the safety to spend the fire

clusters tumbled down
we bagged enough to keep us
kissing through to the New Year,
my mother formed kissing balls

sprigs of holly, ribbon, mistletoe,
gifting aunts, uncles, and cousins,
Our own ball hung from a beam,
we'd switch kisses, sister to sister,

parent to child, although parent
to parent, sadly not so much. Yet
passion there was each day in the small
ways, ways not seen even if we aimed to

Invincibility

On River Road we flew our spirits,
  aboard a Flexible Flyer, still tagged from
Roses', sparks flying from red

runners as we struck gravel. I'd flung
onto my friend's back, time after time,
until we veered into a barbed fence.

Thirty stitches branded Susan's face,
and I, with my mere three, remembered
screaming by the side of the road. Whether I was

Susan's siren or just my own, I don't
recall, yet for the time we were angels, who
still had not forgotten how to fly.

Pond

In a flat-bottom boat
   with my father, fishing,
the sun on my back
and on his face
and in the pond
striders shimmying on the water,
pressing dimples on the surface

It's a slip of presence
I've polished over and over
It nibbles unexpectedly
on a line I'd forgotten was there

We paddle farther out
oar thunking against the boat
magnified in the quiet
tiny funnels swirling
how deep they go

Fish smell, wet warm
wood, tick-tick-tick
of the reel, my father's
mouth curving in a smile
and the one I give back

Brown Mountain Lights

From Wiseman's View lights glided up
and down the sides of the mountain –
ball lightning, St. Elmo's fire, moonshine
stills, ghosts of slain Catawba warriors.

I helped my father bury potatoes in a cave;
Our lantern held together more than the world.
I stood steady with a basket as he hoed.

If you were to begin now – go, sit in your cave –
each will-o-the-wisp would be understood,
the light metaphor would shatter all things,
freeing us from the labor before us.

But Venus rises indifferently with no offer
of help. We must dig in our uncertainty.
Orbs are there and God lends a hoe.

My Father's Fancy

Not a word was said, only Daddy,
smoking and gazing into trees, and me,
ferns arching over our laps and legs.

We had ridden through these woods
before, never stopping, but this once
we dismounted at twilight to rest.

The horses picked at fronds while
the woods around our tiny grove
changed with the light. The oaks receded

like visions of heaven with voices coming
and moving away. That's all I remember.
To conjure a face or thoughts exchanged

is like trying to hum my own story,
robbing the distilled moment:
elbow-deep in an island of ferns

like the time he knelt to my height,
took my small fists in his, and shook my arms
to make the north winds blow.

A lineage came alive in every branching
instinct he acted on. What gleaned things
memories are, like offspring, bare-boned, thriving.

Visitor

The raccoon came to the window
night after night, peering in about
the time we said grace.
Who knew if it watched us gnawing
drumsticks or just saw its own reflection,
but Daddy set a trap,
a hollow log with peanut-butter bait.
"Could be rabid," he said. We talked
about it for weeks, our proper purpose being
to pay attention. Daddy never could bring
himself to give us the exquisite tail.

How It Begins

The tube legs shifted up and down
   in the four corners of the swing set
as a thick-coming fancy came,
unstoppable, from the trees,
like wind in the face and skirt –
If God made me than who made God?
The deity in me did not know, not yet,
that the pebble dropped in hopscotch
is the same as the one in the shoe and the rub is:
God made God in the thought on the swing.

Down the Road

Daddy dressed the squirrel
on a tree, slicing blood gristle
flesh, while we leaned, transfixed,
on our bikes. When he was done,
we shoved off; playing cards
fluttered in the spokes
as fast as heartbeats.

Later, over stew, we fought
about who got the tail. Until the next
rain, blood in the bark resembled
a face, eyeing the sacred ornament
flying from the handlebars
of the girl catching breaths
in an anxious wind.

A bird called from the woods.
She turned to hear what
she wanted to remember and one day
put a name to. Until then nothing
anyone could give her would be
greater than finding ease
in her own skin again.

Tobacco Roads

To think on Pixie Lee's grandma riding the Parkway, you'd swear she's the oldest woman alive. If you rode in their new Ford car, you'd hear her hawk up something into a orange juice can, the likes of which looked like slugs. Pixie Lee had blown a bubble, not worried for the life of her granny, who'd turned her face to see the flyblown world passing by.

Granny said something about a Coky-Cola as we rolled into a filling station paved with bottle-caps, RC, Cheerwine, Bubble-Up, Crush. "You'uns, wait here, I'll git you a poke," and she come back with a bag of jawbreakers and candy cigarettes that Pixie Lee hoarded, handing me one like a Democratic candidate. Granny started in about the Old North State as if

she'd been there when it joined the union. "I been all over," she said, "the highlands, piedmont, sandhills." She pointed out a small barn. "Don't matter where you are, you see them curing sheds, tall and narrow like that. I speck this place's a tree farm now." When we reached our destination, Mystery Hill, she took a swig of Cola, "Hoo-ee, must be

a hun'ert-degree hotter 'n hell." We piled out of the car, but she wouldn't set foot in the crooked house, said she was doing good to stand upright on flat land, so she didn't

behold a ball rolling uphill or water flowing backwise, referred
to as "gravitational anomalies." Later in the car, I told Pixie
Lee she was an anomaly unto herself. Granny sung, *I'll

Fly Away*, and you'd thought, open that window and you just
might. Then she started in on End Times – "The moon'll turn
red, Jesus'll gallop in on a white steed, and blood'll run
deeper
than the hind hock of a horse" – giving Pixie and me the
heebie-jeebies. Two days later, Jesus did come for Pixie Lee's
granny, putting to mind the fresh grave we'd seen at Mystery

Hill with boots waggling out of the dirt. I'd expect if you
wanted to find out where her granny's own grave was, she'd
tell you, "No use to it, I ain't there nohow." And furthermore
she'd inform you, "Be ready when the Big Morning comes."
That's just the way Pixie Lee's granny was.

willard

Chance, for Willard, was a lifestyle. Like the snake
around his neck which he used to frighten
high school girls in penny-loafers
and arouse the ire of the pharmacist at Dayvault's.
Some days, in Indian headdress, he'd parade

the sidewalk, past the Guarantee, past men
in suits and women in shirtwaist dresses,
so predictable in their looking-away way.
He cast to an audience, never his,
recoiling into dusk until a new day.

Cross-References

We didn't understand what my friend's dad
was building in the basement with cinderblocks
but we liked watching. We liked the smell.
Later we learned it was a fallout shelter –
we'd missed bomb drills by a year or so.
A decade later I'd ask to see what I could find
in *National Geographics* stored there, scanning
yellow spines with a flashlight like an archeologist
or miner, surprised to find what I needed
on Dunkirk, Greek life, or B. F. Skinner.
Back in daylight I felt optimistic, as if a bright new
adventure lay ahead, like everything was getting away
and bearing me into the wild blue.

At Nine: Shooting Baskets

I outgrew my mama
when I found out she
wished she'd married another man.

And I thought, Fine, you'd be happier.
But wait, I wouldn't be me
now would I?
Woosh.

On Finley Bald Mountain

As one day of summer passed another and
light gently shifted toward fall, we hauled
out the camp box and jumped into the Jeep.

To our special place, remote, so mountain-
closed yet opened to the sky, we drove to
a site near the swollen stream, untangled

poles and ropes and pitched our pup tent.
We did not hear in the rushing sound
a solitary hint of how quickly life itself

was pressing along its course. But beyond
this life, this world, we'll have this to our
heart's content, a memory: crossing the

summer stream with such joy, eyeing our
separate paths of stones, each stone shouting,
"Now!" and five of us, leaping.

John's River

We fly fish on John's River,
　　Daddy and I, casting our lines
in long arcs over the
bony river

The dog seeks scents,
hole to hole, snuffling
I forget about him
watching striders and the line

When the sun's sunk and
we've packed our tackle, he's gone
we whistle and call until
a burst of hound halts at the shore

Daddy says, "He'll come,"
and heads for the Willys Jeep
"He'll come," but I cry at how
the dog balks on the opposite shore

I can't comprehend this forsaking
but Daddy foresees the plunge
a head, dog-eared, on the water
and even me, fretting on the shore

Bodies of Water

The city pool was our favorite swimming hole,
bright, loud, with frozen Zero bars at the candy
counter. With integration, Daddy said, "No more,"
establishing an image that prevailed all summer:

white girls getting pregnant by swimming sperm.
So, full of no-cares, we swam in the pond, paddling
out, jumping in and climbing out, trying to keep
the boat balanced until thunderstorms broke,

spewing out the South's awful mistakes. Seeing
the first drops, expanding in concentric circles,
we heave-hoed to shore, knowing kids at the pool
were as waterlogged as we and lit up like halos.

Sex Ed in the South

We saw *Tiger Lily,* my friend
and me, down at the Avon.
It had nothing to do
with tigers or lilies.
We never made it to the end.
I told my mother
what we saw – a woman stepping
from the bath, naked in front
of a man – and about
my tickly feeling "down there."
Her answer may as well been Clorox
measured in the wash or a faucet
dripping double time. Honey, maybe
you just need to bathe, could be
why you're itching there.

1966

There was something about that year,
sixth grade in Miss Lackey's room.
I had painstakingly drawn the Taj Mahal
while we listened to war news.
She said she hoped I'd travel one day.

The window shades had pulls Stewart Little
could've swung on. The live oak in the
yard turned yellower every day, its tire swing
dangling like a ring pull, and the flagpole clanged on
the breeze as she read from *The Merchant of Venice*.

She had elephantiasis and so, her enormous legs,
enlarged head, protruding features,
caused us to ponder in silence
how a mere mosquito could do this.
But never did we speak an unkind word about her. Not once.

Janie

She stepped from woods, wearing leggings, plain
smock, rubber boots, jabbing a stick in a puddle;
she was five and wandering the road after rain.

With braids and freckles, the girl down the lane
sold lemonade from a roadside stand,
at nine and wandering the road after rain.

At the pool, the staring boys could hardly explain
the radiant something that whirled around them,
at fifteen and wandering the road after rain.

In the light that settled from the windowpane,
she lifted her face from *The Roman Way,*
at twenty-one and wandering the road after rain.

She lived in the mountains when first the pain
of cancer fell like pebbles of hail across the ridge,
at forty and wandering the road after rain.

How careless death is when children remain,
having lost their umbrella against a storm,
at forty-four and wandering the road after rain.

Had she moved through the years, she'd sustain
that honest look, lifting grandchildren on her knee,
at seventy-five and wandering the road after rain.

We accept time's economy, though we complain,
packing in our hearts those we wish to live on,
stealing from death and from the roads wet with rain.

We keep the way welcoming, washed softly again and again,
that leads from windows, woods, and pools,
where all of us wander the road after rain.

Reactions

Heading home from fields, your words
slurred and you staggered. I led you into
darkening pines and settled you on the ground,
raced home for anything sweet to feed you.
In my twelve years I'd seen you go into diabetic comas,
my father, yet not my father, here, but not
here: I waited while your blood sugar pulled
you back and wondered, always wondering,
where you went.

The Photographer

Daddy aimed a camera in certain uncertain ways,
capturing one of his girls scissor-legging a fence,
dwarfed by mountains. Another daughter held

a fly-rod and squinted from a corner of a black
pool. My mother, in a courtyard in the French Quarter,
glanced treeward, and Daddy caught mostly brick.

He did not aim as through a rifle, but rather
obliquely, not altogether carelessly. The aperture
can fix a pose so image-impelled as to miss

the larger picture. Pinning down the sum of who
we were was not his art, as it was not
his way to miss a fragile falling-into-place.

A Marriage

Don't recollect much touching.
    No hand to the shoulder, leaning in
to the other. Never holding hands
nor swapping kisses.

How surprising then to open a door
on them once, lovemaking. Mama
flung the covers over Daddy's head.
Too late. She'd already opened
a window, a fat cherub flying
through with a secret smile.

Next day it was back to never-exchange.
She carried a basket on her hip, down
past roses to the clothesline. But
all day sheets snapped in the air.

Moon

Our father played "Beautiful Dreamer"
some nights while we waited for sleep,
watching the moon in the window with
its misty ring and few stars inside, signaling

it could snow in a day or so. Would you
rather die in a fire or freeze to death? you'd
ask from your bed, and each childhood
year our answer remained the same.

What we knew so far we could not define:
it was wondrous and alive, like God or
as good as. While we slept the wind
stalked over Hibriten. We awoke

to find the world utterly white. Outside
we flung out our arms, looking upward,
allowing ourselves to disappear and reappear,
far from any fire but burning all the same.

Still Frame

I never wanted blizzards to end
One or two good ones came each year,
and I willed them for all they were worth

Whichever child first discovered the way
the light altered her room would be the one
to wake Daddy on such mornings

He'd spring out of bed as if to throw open
the sash, a kid again, with widened eyes
and a hoo-boy, wouldja-look-at-that

Years later when he was in the hospital
the doctor stood in the doorframe, speaking
in hushed tones. It had started to snow

I watched it falling in the window
beyond his bed, desiring by sheer focus,
to keep it going

Grace

Our cattle always got loose;
   as if the bottoms weren't enough,
they lit out for the hill,
scraping by any barbed barrier.

My mother grabbed a bull by
the horns, not proverbially either,
and tugged it barnward. A neighbor,
spying her, dashed out with rope.

"Good Lord, Laura, that bull could
spear you to death!" God must temper
wind to the shorn lamb because she
never did stop yanking bulls.

At Mother's Knee

She dragged us
>   to every damn antique store
>   in western Carolina
>   to learn what had value
>   and what was junk.

Spinning wheels,
>   depression glass,
>   *Gone with the Wind* lamps
>   were collectibles,
>   that is, tacky.

English antiques
>   were preferable to American.
>   French country was trendy.
>   Pine and white oak,
>   unless quarter-sawn,

looked like old school furniture
>   or yellow church pews.
>   English oak was refined
>   and elegant.
>   Cherry, though soft,

easily scratched,
> was beautiful,
>> as was walnut.
>>> Maple, you painted, like ash,
>>>> and neither had pretty grain.

Grain's important. Bear that in mind.
> Take mahogany,
>> mahogany was good.
>>> Avoid veneers.
>>>> Go for solids.

The North had the money.
> The South had the taste.
>> Insist on ten percent off
>> and remember,
>>> never trust a dealer.

This Southern Thing about Shoes

No white shoes or belts
before Memorial Day
or after Labor Day.
Shoes should match
your purse.
No sling-backs in winter;
patent leather in spring
and summer only.
Shoes should be darker
than your hose, and
no hose with an open toe.
Shoes and skirt of the same color
make your legs look longer
but flats with long skirts
look frumpy.

A final word about shoes:
you never want them
to be the first thing
people notice.

The Other Line

"How's Happy?"
"She spent March in a psych ward."
My mother, on the other line, "Eh, law."
I drew a breath, should I hang up?
I knew better than to eavesdrop
Only wanted to call a friend.

I remembered the name from
an old Christmas card with
five snowmen with human faces
stick-hand in stick-hand
their names beneath: Somebody, somebody,
somebody, somebody, and Happy.
I'd wanted that name.
She looked my age.

My mother launched into our troubles
my pregnant sister and hurried wedding plans
repainting, dress fittings, invitations.
More exchanges of college days, then
a final quiet, "I love you, John." And then
the "me too." I'd hung up two seconds too late

My face flushed, I headed for the woods,
my go-to woods. The day had gone
perfectly well, as did most days. But
suddenly this one grew complex.
I counseled myself, aloud. My father –
did he know? Should I tell someone?

A shining creek, a yellow leaf catching
currents, my heart journeying alone.
Mama and Daddy, both gone now,
and John Whomever, gone too, no doubt.
What did I tell myself back then? At fifteen,
how did I comfort myself?

My parents, though they never parted,
were rarely happy. Back then so many days
lay ahead they'd never run out. Now they rush.
I still take to the woods, counsel
and occasionally embarrass myself
with self-chatter. I ask, how's happy?
She's good.

A Book of My Father's

What is deep longing
but this book inscribed
to my father by a woman who
was not my mother

A book of love poems where
some margins were more
acid-pocked than others
marking thorn-points

A secret core's in everyone,
a most alive moment was
when he knew why she
sent it and why he closed it

Appalachian Spring

Spring in the mountains, and I am on the woodshed.
   You are chopping below. Your mallet strikes sharp notes,
splintering green wood. On my back, I aim an Instamatic
at a clip of a moon. You will soon come out from your work.

I will call, "Daddy," and you'll turn, surprised,
as I catch your half smile, and this image, you
with your bucket of bone meal, will comfort me one day,
while waiting to see your longed-for, upturned face.

Foundering

The gelding barged the feed room
found sweet grain and gorged.
He would not have stopped
if I hadn't found him.

Dr. Thuss put him on Bute, 10cc.
and placed his hooves in buckets of ice.
My job was to keep him standing,
to reduce fever in his feet.

I stayed all night, listening,
feeling warm breath, the steady in and out,
too young to wonder, who'd be with me
if I too might one day founder?

The next day I mucked the stall
God and the horse knew how much!
But I took good care, finding
mindfulness has its sweet reward.

Racing Forbidden Fields

We couldn't resist the haying fields,
the longest run in the county,
though we knew the owner on the hill
would call the police. It was summer.

Our horses sensed the thrill, lifting
muzzles and flinging hooves, while
wind blared its indifference and grass
whipped our stirrups. We made an arc

for the return, spying the squad car,
and doglegged into a cornfield
until the deputy, figuring it didn't take
a sledge to smash a fly, drove off.

Trail Home

There, autumn deepened as my horse went on and on,
leaves drifting all about. Up ahead, a possum scaled
a tree, halted and somersaulted to the ground.
I knew its game and let my horse graze trailside,

snapping heads off goldenrod, while a woodpecker
hammered in the distance. Determined to wait it out,
I wondered why we forget the mystery of watchfulness,
to have nothing more to do than catch a possum peeking.

Touring Tremont

Daddy has gone downhill,
    demanding to go home when he is home.
My mother out, I don't know
what to do but take him for a spin,

through the green-filled neighborhood, past The Crying
Tree and The Sad House in the orchard we
call The Morningside. We see The Far Hill
at the base of Hibriten Mountain and the one lone
chestnut tree still standing, though dead, in a field.

Back in the drive, he's satisfied we're home.
He sighs, everything's the same, he says,
except for the damn black dog
curled on the mat at the door.

Shapes of Attention

The horses in the paddock
will amble through
the shadows to the barn,
and the old man, he will climb the stairs
again to his sister, sick with cancer
while the moon hovers outside.
The clouds will ease their way
across its muffled face.
He will lift the walker, step by step,
creaking, dragging his own bent weight
a million miles and back,
to the bump bump of his steady
high-top shoes on the risers.

This is my father, who loved Mary,
who once rode horses with her, laughing
together from a vivid sense of the world.
Soon Mary's horses will stand nearer
the hammock, nose-to-nose, as if
knowing, as we do, how night climbs
and how nothing falls apart in its descent
but only rises and rises, certain as the moon.

Braided Rug

I changed your urine-soaked socks
and cringed, not from your swollen feet
or smell, but from the language
of your pain, your steady eh law, eh law.

My toes gripped the rug as I unfurled
fresh socks. The way light fell into the room
I knew I'd carry the memory like
a bent photo, seeing myself at sixteen

again when you were seventy, decades
older than my friends' fathers. I'd look
first for you, who was gone. Again,
at me in the picture, forever partly yours.

Under Shade

My mama found The Crying
Tree in the woods behind our house,
where she'd go to be alone or grieve

I went there once, I don't recall
why, when I was six or seven
and saw a funeral procession
at the foot of our hill

I panicked and thought my father
had died. Finding no one home
I ran to my friend's house but
didn't ask. I trusted their normalcy

and relaxed in my skin
and later found my father
chopping wood. Children need
dress rehearsals, I suppose

He died thirteen years later
after a long illness, my grief, though
intense, was two-thirds complete
expectancy having kept apace

Bascom Storey

To hear Mama tell it, Bascom Storey could stay
longer in an hour than any person on earth.
Daddy'd kept him out of prison, which is why
Bascom came for years to visit, bearing beans,
greens, fatback, or firewood.

So what are all these lawyers doing in our kitchen
now? Where were they when Daddy was sick?
High-stepping roosters in mud. And though
Bascom didn't come to the memorial service,
in his stained coveralls and straw hat, only he,
I think, really knew how to remember.

Birthdays

When I turned eleven I got Charmin Chatty
and for my twelfth, a sled, shiny and red
at thirteen, a sweater, gloves—a slight letdown—
and a diary with a tiny key

My 7th grade friends threw me a surprise
party. Homemade signs with "Happy 13th,
Smiley!" my new nickname
We swam, played spin-the-bottle,

pairing off to practice kissing,
my "date" and I, in the dark
not daring to move but I was happy
Then changes came so fast

my father broke his foot, later his hip
after that, early-onset dementia
Sisters left for college or married
and on my sixteenth my mother

organized a surprise party with friends,
who by then had taken to calling me,
"Moody." I laughed a bit at
the card that opened to a little

bag of screws, wires, and bolts
"to build your own car," admired
the already-black mood ring, inhaled
Wind Song, feeling awkward, sad

My seventeenth, friends and I, silly
and giddy, dyed food in the refrigerator:
blue milk, pink cottage cheese, yellow
whip cream, green yogurt

Five months after my father died,
my mother took me to a trattoria where
an accordion player sang "Happy Birthday."
Mortification on my nineteenth

So many birthdays since, decades,
love demonstrated to me every time
bliss and pain wrapped together with rich
associations unique to me and treasured

Inheritance

He gave measure to the things he left:
a fishing rod, binoculars, garden tools,
his mother's painting, and a satin quilt,

as if without him his daughters might take
up his pastimes and still be with him.
But all I could think of was how we rode

to The Far Hill, dismounted, and sat
in ferns, listening to a bobwhite.
At sunset we set out for Elephants Grave.

Mimicking him, I outstretched my arm
to an orange sun and sang out a mournful
chant, filling up with a holy presence.

Mother and Child

At five I showed you my painting.
You said it resembled Joseph's coat.
Who's that? I asked. Intending no shame,
you said you couldn't believe I didn't know.
I would have liked to have known.

Twenty-five years later we drove past
St. Stephen's. Never heard of Stephen
you commented. I said he was the first
martyred disciple. If I knew something,
I could've been making it up.

How might we have made better
exchanges? Handing one another
stones, it was often the same:
Intending no shame not many
ever turned to bread.

Wry Soul

Sick with heart disease, my mother was
not always entirely herself. In some ways
she was better than herself.

Her last Halloween, dressed in a man's suit,
she drove to a party at the beautiful
old home on Beale Street.

Friends gathered, mostly widows –
sorceresses, clowns, opera singers,
but no one recognized my mother.

Fedora, cigar, five-o-clock shadow –
who was that fragile-looking man
in the big suit, mute in the armchair?

Or when I called from Norway, not many
months later, she was full of news
about the lawn and humidity.

Mother, I said finally, I'm calling from
the Arctic Circle – at $10 a minute.
I sensed her wan smile a world away. Well,
whatever is the weather like there, dear?

Maypops

Mama yanked weeds around the fence
where passion flowers grew,
opening at sunrise, closing at sunset.
We gathered fleabane.

Mama swept wisps of hair from her brow
and picked a blossom from the vine,
plucked its stamens and showed us
a tiny ballerina.

Her last year she came home in a truck
loaded with snow and hospital flowers.
Over her shoulder through frosted glass,
she peered out at this oddest of beds.

Stories My Mother Told

You told me about the time, dashing to school,
you tripped into a ditch, disturbed a rabbit's nest
and kittens erupted and leapt all over you.
That happened over seventy years ago – a small

sunlit moment in your life. You're gone now, but
the marvel could live on. My children might tell
their children about you laughing and rolling in
the leaf-filled ditch.

Once, mowing, I hit a rabbit's nest and the babies
spewed out from the blades, unharmed, except one
that lost an ear. From time to time, we'd see it, one-eared,
in the yard. Just to prove things live on, I wrote this.

Colors

My mother's bedroom changed colors
through the years. Early on it was brown
with white trim. I napped on a nubby
coverlet that left an imprint on my face,
the same brass bed I jumped on the day

Kennedy was shot. I had scarlet fever
when the room was blue. Sheers billowed
on a breeze that wouldn't cool me.
Dr. McNairy blew up a balloon, rubbed it on
my head and made it stick to the wall.

The room was wallpapered after my father
died. Home from college, I read *The First
Circle* while an Irish Setter snored on a yellow
rug. During Mama's illness, it was white
and aqua. Toward the end, I watched her

sleeping through the half-closed door.
Dogwoods in bloom reached through
the window to take me back to Easters,
when we lay in bed, ate jellybeans, and peered
into sugared eggs at the tiniest of scenes.

When I Got Drunk with My Mother

Let me tell you about the winter I was nineteen.
My father had died and I didn't know why
we were going to a party, but my friends were to be
there and so were hers.
We drank in different parts of the house.
Eventually my friends left but my mother
and I stayed until the wee hours.

She looked young and pretty then. Over her
shoulder a window held our reflections.
Indistinguishable. My eyes started seeing through
things, my old self through a new self. Though hard
to describe, I saw with better ideas. Back and forth from her
to the glass, I loved her, mysteriously, newly.

Cabin

Listen. What I have to tell
is that the world we knew is gone.
Just as the stack of logs
we loved burned down
so many years ago. I'm inclined
to speak about it because what
we had didn't peel off like the bark
our mother swept away and away.
Remember the ball lightning
bowling through the kitchen,
knocking Daddy down
and the mice droppings
in our beds like caraway seeds?
You don't need to be there
to be there. You don't need to own it
to have it. We carry those days
wherever we go. They open up
like this and fire balls fly.

Seeking What Won't Change

I have moved along old paths
    again and again,
entering different lives in our house
    among trees on the wide curve.
Beneath the gold canopy, leaves dropped
    where the mind goes blank
and a split-rail fence led the eye down
    to the school, to the red-clay playground.
Certain playmates came to life. Dale Brown,
    killed on his bike in front of the school.
Camille, who lived above a gas station.
    The girl whose dishwater curls I coveted,
whose clapboard house light shown
    clear through.
It never occurred to me who was richer
    or poorer until my teacher let slip
she thought we thought we were
    better than others.
Passing years in a single moment was
    like finding a marble on the playground,
in a million motions you pick it up,
    spit to clear the cat's eye,
foggy but dilated still.

Child Maps

Fallen trees on The Far Hill
crisscross the trails
remnants of Hugo in '89
but the lay of the land
is still in my head every dip
and bend in the hills
and hollows, the best
place to canter or let the horse
graze, best view
of the pond
copse of white pines
groves of fern
scent of humus
thicket and pine
I know them by heart
they're still in my head
nothing can bear them away

Paths Before We Knew Them

I call it the Easter-
of-myself dream. Climbing
Tremont Hill homeward,
watching myself cross my arms
over my chest and dying
to the ground.

How long it's stayed with me,
fifty-two years, the way I
said "yes" to Altitude
and saw my spirit rise
as my body dropped
to the ground.

The word and look
and movement from a
single dream spoke:
Reach upward with no end,
those who don't,
wander on the ground

Acknowledgments

There's a Jewish story that before the time of your birth God takes you to a field of bundles. Each bundle is filled with troubles, and you have to choose one to take with you to Earth. The story goes that at the time of your death, if God were to take you back to the field to pick another bundle with which to relive your life, you would choose the same bundle.

Troubles are always easier to bear when you can share them, and since the flipside of trouble is joy, I'd need to start by thanking my husband, who has brought me much joy in my life. Bob Hudson, best friend, soulmate, kind critic, and encourager, has loved my poems and pushed me to keep at it. I'm fortunate to have him as a literal in-house editor and amazing book designer.

Even though my parents have long departed, they remain as near to me as breath. Laura and Folger Townsend, thank you for deep roots and even deeper values. They've sustained me through tough times.

I'm grateful for my children, who brought my own childhood into relief and caused me to enter into the adventurous and magical realm of childhood a second time. They were my teachers then as they are now.

The child is mother of the woman. I'm grateful for having had the freedom, stability, and nurturance to be a child, a teenager, a young adult, and now an older woman.

Shelley at age six

Shelley Townsend-Hudson

Shelley Townsend-Hudson was born in Lenoir, North Carolina. Her father, a small-town attorney, a gentleman farmer, and a lover of poetry, named her in honor of poet Percy Bysshe Shelley. Her father was a friend of Thomas Wolfe at the University of North Carolina in 1919.

Shelley's childhood home was on a road called Tremont Circle, which wound around a hill at the foot of Hibriten Mountain, just east of Lenoir.

Today she is a musician, a dancer, and an award-winning poet. Her poems have appeared in various literary journals and in a series of chapbooks published by the Perkipery Press.

Shelley sings and plays banjo in the old-time string band Gooder'n Grits, which performs for dances and festivals throughout west Michigan.

She enjoys showing her Welsh Terrier, Brynmawr Sweet Tea and Cornbread, in AKC and UKC conformation classes, barn hunt, and tracking.

She is married to author Robert Hudson, and they have three daughters, Abbie, Molly, and Lili. Shelley and Robert split their time between Ada, Michigan, and Old Salem, North Carolina.

www.ingramcontent.com/pod-product-compliance
Lightning Source LLC
Chambersburg PA
CBHW070241090526
44586CB00035B/1369